THEY PLAY WHAT?!

The Weird History of Sports and Recreation

Richard Platt

TWO CAN™

MINNETONKA, MINNESOTA

Contents

First published in the USA in 2007 by
Two-Can Publishing
11571 K-Tel Drive
Minnetonka, MN 55343
www.two-canpublishing.com

Editorial Director: Jill Anderson
Editor: Nadia Higgins
Cover Design: Brad Norr Design

ISBN 978-1-58728-585-1 (HC)
ISBN 978-1-58728-586-8 (PB)

Library of Congress Cataloging-in-Publication Data on file

1 2 3 4 5 11 10 09 08 07

Printed in China

WARNING: The activities in this book are for information only and should not be tried at home!

- 4-5   Ancient Pastimes
- 6-7   Roman Games
- 8-9   War Games
- 10-11   Pistols at Dawn
- 12-13   Eastern Arts
- 14-15   Run for It
- 16-17   On the Ball
- 18-19   Kicking, Throwing, Rolling
- 20-21   Faster Than a Speeding Snail
- 22-23   Beastly Pleasures
- 24-25   A-Hunting We Will Go
- 26-27   At the Circus
- 28-29   Falling Fast
- 30-31   Water Sports
- 32-33   Taking to Air
- 34-35   Land Daredevils
- 36-37   Nice Ice
- 38-39   Feats of Endurance
- 40-41   Shall We Dance?
- 42-43   Celebrations Around the Year
- 44   What's So Weird About That?
- 45   Find Out More
- 46-48   Glossary and Index

Introduction

WHAT DO YOU DO FOR FUN and to relax? Perhaps you play a computer game or read a book. Maybe you watch TV or kick around a ball with friends. Have you ever thought about trying something a little different? How about going to watch two slaves fight to the death? Or what about dressing in a tin suit and hurtling along on horseback in a mock battle?

These sports from the past seem weird now, but centuries ago they were respectable ways of spending an afternoon. For fun, people also tried flying through the air like birds or sliding down hills on ice blocks. Today we have improved on some of these ancient amusements—and we've thought of other equally strange or dangerous games.

Extreme sports, for instance, double the danger of your favorite sport. Difficult or downright deadly, games like **BASE jumping** or speed skiing push at the boundaries of what is possible—and legal. Other new games, like ostrich or pig racing, are harmless but silly. In the pages that follow, you can read about all these peculiar pastimes and learn how they grew to be popular.

Would You Believe...?

What, where, why, who? What was the punishment for hunting in the king's forests? Where can you see bog-**snorkeling** races? Why did the crowds run away from the Mayan ball-game stadium every time there was a goal? Who invented hang gliders? To find out the answers, read on!

Ancient Pastimes

Prehistoric games ▶
Carved from wood or shaped from clay, animal figures have always delighted small children. This wood tiger is from a tomb in Thebes, on the Nile River. An Egyptian child played with it about 3,500 years ago. It may have lost a leg, but its glinting glass eye and string-operated jaw give the beast an authentic snarl.

PEOPLE FROM THE DISTANT PAST had little time for play. Even children worked hard. Before they were old enough to speak, children could scare birds from growing crops. When they did have time to relax, their toys were simple but similar to the ones many small children play with today—balls, dolls, animals, and wheeled toys.

Would You Believe...?

Aztec wheels
The **Aztec** people of ancient Mexico made wheeled toys, but they never used wheeled vehicles. Some experts say this was because carts and carriages were useless without animals to pull them. There were no horses in Mexico until Europeans brought them in 1519.

We know about these ancient toys and games mainly because archaeologists (people who study the remains of past worlds) have found traces of them in graves and tombs. Egyptian tombs contain many toys, preserved by the dry desert air.

◀ **First dolls?**
Figuring out who made the first dolls is a tricky business. Many ancient peoples made small human figures for use in religious ceremonies but not as toys. Some figures may have had both uses. The Hopi Indians of present-day Arizona made brightly painted *kachina* figures such as this one to use in worship. Later they would pass the objects on to their children.

Instead of dice, children in ancient Greece threw astragals—the square ankle bones of pigs and other animals.

Organized games and sports have a very long history, too. The **Olympic Games** began in the ancient city of Olympia, Greece, in 776 B.C. Naked athletes competed for a crown of leaves—and the glory of winning. These first Olympic Games were part of a religious festival. There was a break from the races for the **sacrifice** (religious killing) of 100 cattle.

▲ **From nuts to marbles**
More than 2,000 years ago, Roman children played the game of "nuts" by rolling hazelnuts, rounded pebbles, or specially made glass balls. They weren't the first to play marbles, though. Egyptian children had used clay balls for similar games many centuries before. Marbles were given their modern name when they were made from marble rock in the 18th century.

Roman Games

ARMED WITH SIMPLE, SAVAGE weapons, two warriors enter a huge arena. The pair fight for their lives. As the loser's blood spills out onto the hot sand, 50,000 people cheer the victor! It sounds like a gory computer game, but it's not. To the people of Rome 2,000 years ago, deadly battles like this were popular spectator sports.

Called *munera*, the battles were part of the Roman games that also included chariot races, theatrical shows, and wild animal hunts. The fighters, called **gladiators,** were slaves, prisoners of war, or criminals. The most successful became heroes, just like today's star athletes.

● ● ● ● ● ● ● ● ● ● ●

Roman graffiti has been found that praises the gladiator Celadus as "the girls' heartthrob."

▲ **Mock naval battles**
From time to time, the arena was filled with water, and gladiators staged naval battles.

▼ **Matched warriors**
Gladiators were outfitted like actors in a play, and their "costumes" varied. A gladiator took on a role with a special name based on his combination of weapons and **armor.** Here, a *retiarius* (net man) on the left fights his traditional opponent, the *secutor* (chaser).

Not every gladiator fight ended in death. If the loser fought well, the crowd waved handkerchiefs to signal that his life should be spared.

Fish man's helmet ▶
A gladiator's armor couldn't be too skimpy—a quick death spoiled the show! A *murmillo* (fish man) wore a strong helmet with a pierced visor to protect his face. Although this was his only armor, he also gripped a shield to protect his body. A *hoplomachus* (Greek fighter) had a helmet, a large shield, and armor on one arm and leg. A *retiarius*, however, had just one arm protected by armor.

Blind attack
A **jousting** knight could barely see through the thin slit in his helmet. However, he was completely blind at the moment of impact. As he attacked, he tilted his head back. This stopped his foe's **lance** (a long, blunt pole) from forcing open the eye slit, but it also left him fighting blind.

WARFARE IS DEADLY and horrible, and even the victor suffers terribly. War games, though, can be an exciting match of skills, thrills, luck, and pluck. On a computer screen, war games are bloodless battles. In the past they were much more physical!

Dressed in feather costumes, Mexico's ancient Aztec people fought with real weapons to capture their foes. The losers were later sacrificed to the sun god!

Aztec warrior ▶
The best warriors went to battle dressed in whole-body armor shaped like a jaguar or an eagle. Beginners wore hardly more than a loincloth. This image shows a modern Mexican dressed as a warrior for the **Pan-American Games.**

● ● ● ● ● ● ● ● ● ● ● ● ● ● ● ● ● ● ● ●

The Aztecs named their ritual battles flowery wars **because feuding warriors fell like** colorful petals.

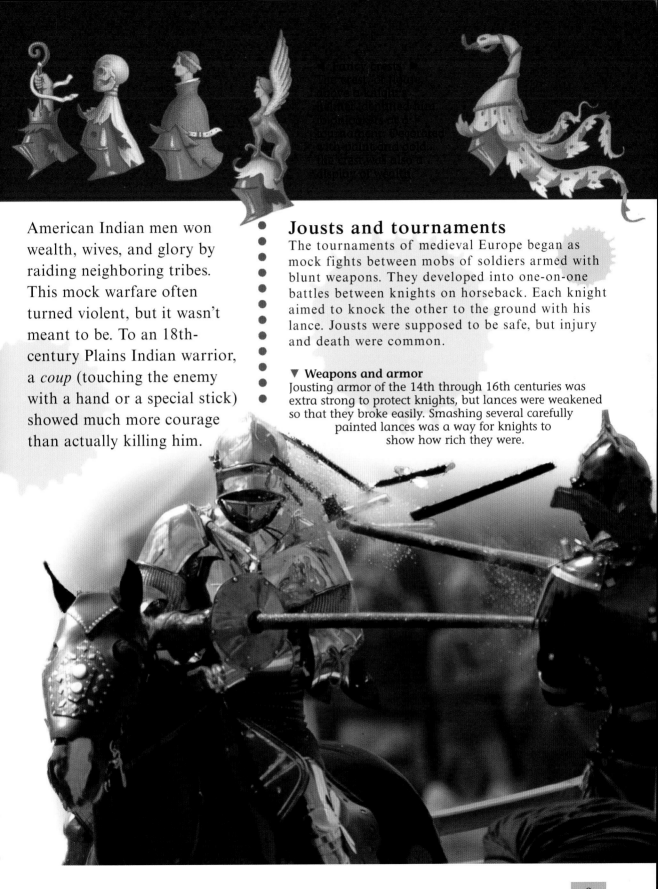

American Indian men won wealth, wives, and glory by raiding neighboring tribes. This mock warfare often turned violent, but it wasn't meant to be. To an 18th-century Plains Indian warrior, a *coup* (touching the enemy with a hand or a special stick) showed much more courage than actually killing him.

Jousts and tournaments

The tournaments of medieval Europe began as mock fights between mobs of soldiers armed with blunt weapons. They developed into one-on-one battles between knights on horseback. Each knight aimed to knock the other to the ground with his lance. Jousts were supposed to be safe, but injury and death were common.

▼ **Weapons and armor**
Jousting armor of the 14th through 16th centuries was extra strong to protect knights, but lances were weakened so that they broke easily. Smashing several carefully painted lances was a way for knights to show how rich they were.

Pistols at Dawn

Would You Believe...?

Go for the red
Perhaps the strangest duel was fought in France in 1843. It took place between two men who had argued over a game of billiards (a game similar to pool). The weapons they chose were billiard balls. The first man to throw landed the red ball on his opponent's forehead, killing him instantly!

H OW FAR WOULD you go to settle an argument? Not long ago you might have challenged the person to a gun battle called a duel. Duels were a legal way for wealthy and important people to settle disputes and get revenge.

Duels began as "trial by combat" 1,500 years ago. When two men both claimed something as their own, they fought to see who would keep it. People believed that God knew the true owner and would decide who won.

The end of duels
Though strict rules governed duels, death was often the goal. This led most countries to ban it. Duels turned into the sports of boxing, wrestling, and fencing, in which both competitors live to fight again!

Fist fighting ▶
The modern sport of boxing began in the 19th century with bare-knuckle prize fights. But fist fights were also popular at the ancient Olympic Games and in ancient Rome, where these figures were made some 2,100 years ago.

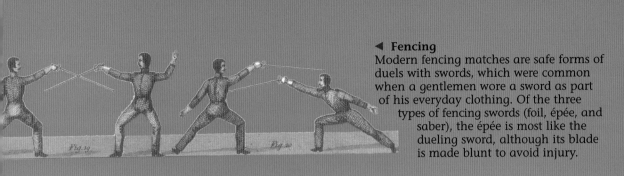

◄ Fencing
Modern fencing matches are safe forms of duels with swords, which were common when a gentlemen wore a sword as part of his everyday clothing. Of the three types of fencing swords (foil, épée, and saber), the épée is most like the dueling sword, although its blade is made blunt to avoid injury.

▲ Dueling pistols
To ensure a fair fight, dueling pistols came in identical sets, like these from 1804. Duelists stood back to back (traditionally at dawn) and took an agreed number of steps before turning to fire. A "second" (a friend and supporter) assisted each duelist and made sure that there was no cheating.

The saying "pistols for two and coffee for one" sums up the deadly end of the duel.

Eastern Arts

WHAT DO YOU GET when you mix warfare with athletics and **philosophy?** Karate, sumo, tae kwon do, judo, and similar sports combine these three components in different ways, making Eastern **martial arts** very different from brutal fights and duels.

In ancient Asia, hand-to-hand fighting was a valuable survival skill. Martial arts became sports only after the invention of guns made them less important for self-defense. Westerners first learned of martial arts through 19th-century stage shows. In recent times, movies have helped to make martial arts popular ways to get fit, get happy— and defend yourself.

Samurai ▶
Martial arts were the trade of Japan's noble warriors, the Samurai, who fought between the 12th and 19th centuries. Shown here as a Japanese theater character, a Samurai actually fought in lightweight armor. The Samurai did use a long sword, but he also trained in unarmed fighting methods including *sumai* and jujitsu.

◄ Sumo wrestling

Twelve centuries ago, Japanese men fought to the death in bouts called *sumai*. Today's sumo wrestlers aim only to push their opponents out of the ring. A fighter's weight counts for a lot, but sumo fans insist that wrestling skills are more important. Here, a grand champion performs a ritual before entering the ring.

Karate kid ▼

There's much more to karate than the wood-splintering "chops" for which it is famous. Meaning "empty hand" in Japanese, karate combines punching, kicking, and striking with the elbow and open hand. Training also involves dance-like sequences called *kata*, which help students to remember moves.

Would You Believe...? Would You Believe...? Would You Believe...?

Heavyweights
All sumo wrestlers are fat, and many weigh as much as 400 pounds (181 kg). To keep up their weight, sumo stars skip breakfast, but they eat a large lunch called *chanko-nabe,* washed down with beer. The wrestlers' diet and lifestyle is unhealthy. Most die ten years younger than other Japanese people.

GASPING FOR BREATH, Pheidippides the messenger stumbled into Athens. Everyone was waiting for news from Marathon, where the Greeks and the Persians were at war. "We were victorious!" he gasped, before dying of exhaustion. His heroic 21-mile (34-km) dash is still celebrated with the **marathon** running race.

Running began as a way to escape savage beasts and to carry messages. But even in Pheidippides' time, 2,500 years ago, it was a sport as well. Today running is among the most popular individual sports. Each year millions compete in races or try to beat their personal best time around the track.

Super sprinter ▲
African-American sprinter Jesse Owens became an international hero at the 1936 Olympics in Berlin, Germany. He finished first in four track events, including the 100-meter and 200-meter sprints. His victory embarrassed Germany's racist Nazi rulers, who claimed that white people were superior to black people. Owens proved them wrong.

The fastest Olympic runners have run at about 22 miles per hour (35 kmph) during the 100-meter and 200-meter sprints.

Modern marathon ▼
Each year, about 800 marathon races are held around the world. With 35,000 competitors, the New York City Marathon is one of the most popular. Few runners finish in less than two and a half hours, but the world record is 25 minutes less than this.

On the Ball

Would You Believe...?

Sorry loser
For players in the **Mayan** ball game *pok-a-tok*, winning was a matter of life or death—literally. Winners became as popular as today's rock stars, while losers were sometimes sacrificed in religious ceremonies. The Mayans probably believed that the sacrifice made the sun shine and the crops grow.

NO TOY IS SIMPLER than a ball, but try and count the different ways of playing with it, and you will soon give up. There are so many kinds of ball games because balls are among the most ancient of toys. Everywhere in the world, you will find a traditional way of playing ball, each with its own rules, perhaps a special ball, and always fanatical fans!

The oldest balls we know of were made in ancient Egypt 3,400 years ago. They were made of carved wood or tightly wound reeds. People everywhere made balls from whatever materials they could find. The first rubber balls came from Central America, where rubber trees grow wild.

Roman games

In the Roman ball game *harpastum*, each team of 5 to 12 players tried to keep the ball in their half of the field for as long as possible. Another Roman favorite, *expulsim ludere*, was a form of handball in which players bounced the ball to each other off the wall of a special court.

◀ ▲ **Volleyball, anyone?** These young Roman women playing ball look remarkably modern. But the artwork in which they appear was created 17 centuries ago in Sicily. Their ball is probably a small *follis*, which had an air-filled animal bladder inside it.

Around the year 1000, the **Vikings** of northern Europe played a rough bat and ball game called *knattleikr* on frozen lakes and ice-covered fields. Ancient Viking folk tales describe vigorous matches that left the ice stained red with blood.

▲ All sorts of balls
Rolling, bouncing, tumbling, or flying in the air, balls come in an endless variety. Balls smaller than an orange are usually for hitting with a stick or paddle. Balls melon-sized and bigger are for kicking or throwing with two hands.

When Europeans arrived in Mexico in the 1500s, they marveled at how high **the Aztec people's rubber balls bounced.**

Mayan games
In Central America's most popular game, players tried to hit a rubber ball through a stone hoop using only their hips, elbows, and knees. The team that scored highest won the clothes and jewelery of all the spectators.

◄ *Pok-a-tok* player
This Mayan pottery figure shows a ball player in action. Kneeling to strike the ball, he wears protective padding around his waist.

Kicking, Throwing, Rolling

WITH 1,000 PLAYERS, a field the size of a small town, and the only rule being "no killing," soccer games in medieval Europe were riotous fun—and sometimes deadly. The game got safer in the early 19th century when schoolboys began to play it. In the United States, soccer developed into the country's favorite sport—football.

▲ Mob game
In Florence, Italy, the *Calcio Storico* ball game mixes soccer and fighting. It began in 1530 as a way to annoy a foreign king whose army was surrounding the city.

Foul play ▶
Soccer has mostly shaken off its deadly past, though as this newspaper picture from 1927 shows, violent tackles continued long after mob games ended.

● ● ● ● ● ● ● ● ● ● ● ● ● ● ● ● ●

The first football game was played on November 6, 1869, in New Jersey. The players used a round, soccer-like ball that was too clumsy to throw. The ball also leaked so much air that the players had to stop the game to blow it up.

TRAGIQUE MATCH DE FOOTBALL

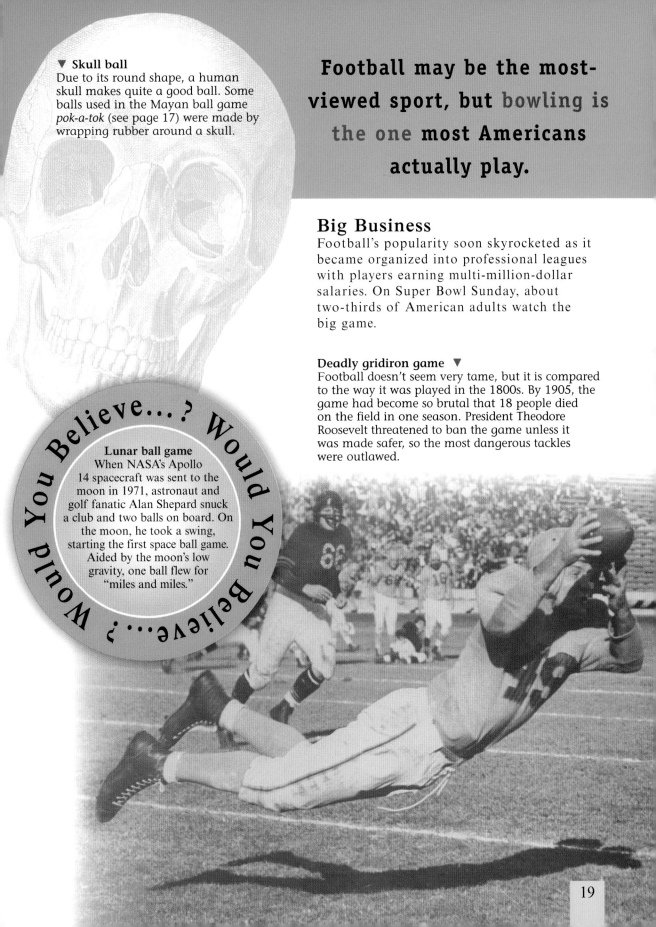

▼ Skull ball
Due to its round shape, a human skull makes quite a good ball. Some balls used in the Mayan ball game *pok-a-tok* (see page 17) were made by wrapping rubber around a skull.

Football may be the most-viewed sport, but bowling is the one most Americans actually play.

Big Business
Football's popularity soon skyrocketed as it became organized into professional leagues with players earning multi-million-dollar salaries. On Super Bowl Sunday, about two-thirds of American adults watch the big game.

Deadly gridiron game ▼
Football doesn't seem very tame, but it is compared to the way it was played in the 1800s. By 1905, the game had become so brutal that 18 people died on the field in one season. President Theodore Roosevelt threatened to ban the game unless it was made safer, so the most dangerous tackles were outlawed.

Would You Believe...? Would You Believe...?

Lunar ball game
When NASA's Apollo 14 spacecraft was sent to the moon in 1971, astronaut and golf fanatic Alan Shepard snuck a club and two balls on board. On the moon, he took a swing, starting the first space ball game. Aided by the moon's low gravity, one ball flew for "miles and miles."

Faster Than a Speeding Snail

THE CROWD ROARS AS THE RACE begin! **Gamblers** wave wads of money as they rush to make last-minute bets. As the racers approach the finish line, there's a disaster. A passing bird snaps up the leading runner. When snails are racing, anything can happen!

Snail racing is just one of the newest and wackiest forms of entertainment. Since ancient times, people have held every kind of race you can think of—and many more you cannot!

Snail's pace ▲
The Internet made snail racing popular when an online gambling site took bets on a race in 2000.

▼ Hump on the move
Camel racing is more popular than horse racing in the Middle East. Wealthy leaders of Arab nations sponsor the sport, one of whom owns 14,000 racing camels.

Would You Believe...?

Robot riders
Camel racing used to support an inhuman practice. Because of their light bodies, boy slaves as young as six were forced to be jockeys. In 2006, new laws made this illegal. Some camels are now ridden by robot jockeys. The robots are controlled by a "trainer" who follows the race in a car!

RACING FACTS

The third annual Pig Olympics, held in Moscow, Russia, in 2006, included running races, swimming races, and pig soccer. Pigs from seven countries took part.

The Story Bridge Hotel in Brisbane, Australia, hosts the world's oldest cockroach race. It was first held in 1982.

The most famous frog race is the Calaveras Frog Jumping Championship, held in California. Two thousand frogs compete once a year to beat the 1986 record of 21.48 feet (6.55 m).

◄ Ostrich racing
These big African birds cannot fly, but they can run at 40 miles per hour (64 kmph). They are strong enough to carry an adult jockey, and racing them is a popular sport on the South African farms where they are raised.

The fastest garden snails can race for the finish line at 8 inches (20 cm) per minute.

The Olympic Games featured horse racing for the first time in 648 B.C.

Racers drove horse-drawn chariots around Rome's giant arena 2,000 years ago while 250,000 Romans cheered from the seats. Racing is thrilling because you never know who will win. Betting adds to the excitement, and is the only reason many races are run.

▲ Racing bacon
Once a game for village parties, pig racing became a big success in Russia in 2006. Farmers breed special racing pigs by choosing parents with long legs. Coaches and psychologists train the piglets at the Sport Pig Center near Moscow for races on a special track later in the year.

Gambling on horse races became so out of control in 17th-century Scotland that limits had to be set. Anyone whose winnings went over the limit had to give the excess to the poor.

The annual Ostrich Festival is held in Chandler, Arizona. Ostrich races are the main attraction—alongside stalls selling ostrich burgers and ostrich-skin boots!

Beastly Pleasures

STRONG, FIERCE, AND QUICK, animals can be fascinating to watch. Today we marvel at their survival skills in wildlife films and cheer them at rodeos. But animal entertainment goes back thousands of years. The Minoan people, of ancient Crete, celebrated the strength of bulls by vaulting over them.

The animals of ancient Rome were not so lucky. Gladiators staged brutal battles with lions and tigers to entertain the crowds. The beasts were so scared that keepers had to use flaming torches to drive them to fight.

▲ Bear baiting
Like many of her subjects, English queen Elizabeth I loved to watch dogs attack a bear chained to a post. The "bait" went on until all the dogs were dead, or the bear was too wounded to fight. Specially built arenas called bear gardens hosted these events from the 11th century until they were banned in 1835.

▼ Minoan bull vaulting
The Minoan people, who lived on the Mediterranean island of Crete some 3,500 years ago, worshipped bulls. Their sculptures show athletes vaulting over bulls' backs and horns. Here, a man (with knees and arms missing) goes head first between a bull's horns.

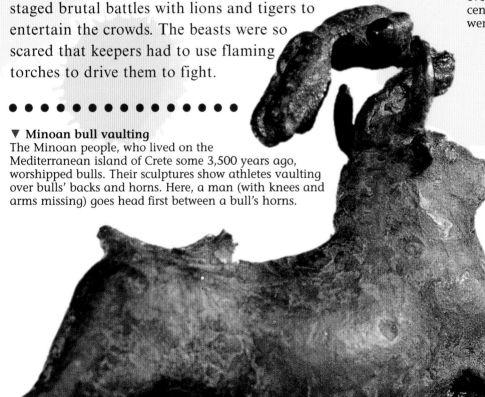

◀ **Dog fighting**
Dog fighting is banned in the United States, but it continues illegally, using breeds such as the Staffordshire and Pit Bull terriers. Not only are these breeds good fighting dogs. Both breeds are used to hunt rats, and "Staffies" make great family dogs.

Secret battles

The Romans eventually tired of their "hunts," but cruel animal sports have never really ended. To entertain crowds and please gamblers, animal keepers have set all sorts of beasts against each other—including ferocious dogs and roosters bred to fight to the death in the ring. Most countries ban these battles, but they still continue in secret.

Would You Believe...? Would You Believe...? Would You Believe...?

Fighting until extinction
In a single Roman arena, gladiators killed up to 5,000 animals in a day. To keep up with this demand, trappers rounded up beasts in Africa and shipped them to Rome. This cruel trade grew so huge that some North African animals became extinct.

▲ **Cock fighting**
Male chickens, or cockerels, are ferocious fighters even in the farmyard, using their spurs (sharp points on their legs) to wound rivals. Gamblers take advantage of the cock's fighting spirit by setting pairs in arenas called cockpits and betting on which will kill the other. Cock fighting is still allowed—and popular—in many countries.

Sharp, long spikes called cockspurs are sometimes attached to the heels of fighting cocks.

23

A-Hunting
We Will Go

FOR CENTURIES, EUROPE'S RICH and powerful people chased deer, pigs, foxes—and almost anything else that ran away—with a meaningless cry of "Tally-ho!" In the Middle Ages (1000–1400), hunting changed the landscape and laws. Kings and queens took the best land for themselves. They punished others who hunted there with torture or death.

Hunting was the only sport considered good enough for members of ruling families. Wealthy noblemen took their favorite hunting hawks to the dinner table and even into the bedroom.

▲ Fox hunting
Like the wolves they resemble, foxes are hunted as pests because they kill farm animals. Medieval hunters chased foxes on horseback with dogs. Such hunts are now illegal in many countries, but foxes can still be shot as pests.

◄ Poaching
Until 1216, peasants bold (or foolish) enough to poach (hunt illegally) in royal forests faced death. The lucky ones might just have had their hands and feet cut off. Even in the 19th century, land owners caught poachers with brutal **mantraps**, as shown on the handle of this hunting sword.

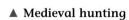

▲ Medieval hunting
The word *forest* originally meant not woodland, but land the king claimed for hunting, as shown in this picture from the 12th century. The animals the king hunted in the forest were fed on crops grown outside the area. The peasants who grew the animal feed were forbidden to hunt the animals.

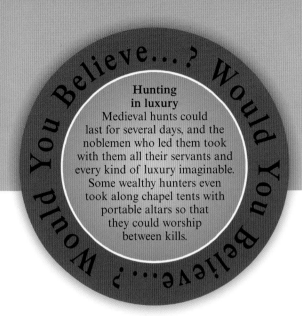

Would You Believe...? Would You Believe...? Would You Believe...?

Hunting
in luxury
Medieval hunts could
last for several days, and the
noblemen who led them took
with them all their servants and
every kind of luxury imaginable.
Some wealthy hunters even
took along chapel tents with
portable altars so that
they could worship
between kills.

The excited barking of a pack of hounds accompanied every hunt.

Hunting with animals

Hawks helped in hunts for small **game** like rabbits, but other tame animals played a big part in all hunts. Hunters could keep up with their prey only on horseback, and they relied on dogs' keen sense of smell to follow the trails of the animals they chased.

Hooded birds ▶
Hunters hooded, or blindfolded, their birds like the one shown here. Then they stroked the birds with feathers. This helped to calm them before a hunt.

● ● ● ● ● ● ● ● ● ● ● ● ● ● ● ● ● ● ●

Traditional hunts generally ended with the death of the animal, so they were called **blood sports.** Many people think hunting is cruel, especially when dogs are used in the chase. In countries where this style of hunting is now banned, hunters can still enjoy the thrill of the chase. They set their hounds to follow a trail laid by dragging a strong-smelling object.

At the Circus

S HOWMAN PHINEAS T. BARNUM loaded his huge circus on to a railway train for its 1872 American tour, boasting that it was "The Greatest Show on Earth." He was probably right. It took 65 trucks to carry the tent, rings, animals, and performers.

Barnum did not invent the circus, though. Englishman Philip Astley first filled a ring with sawdust in 1768. He made the ring 42 feet (13 m) wide because he knew he could stand on the back of a horse trotting around a circle just this big.

▲ Acrobatics
Tricks on horseback amused early circus audiences, along with tightrope and trapeze acts. Frenchman Jules Léotard introduced the first circus trapeze act in 1859.

◄ Animal acts
Circus audiences once expected to watch lions "tamed" in the ring and see other beasts perform tricks, like this boxing kangaroo. Cruelty concerns have put an end to most animal acts.

Would You Believe...?

Famous farter
French baker Joseph Pujol usually performed on stage, but his strange act was perfectly suited to the circus. From 1887 to 1914, he entertained audiences as *Le Pétomane* (The Fartist). His long, odorless farts imitated animals, musical instruments, canons, thunder, and even earthquakes!

The golden age of circus

By 1825, circuses had a winning combination. Under a "big top" (tent), they staged strange and wonderful acts. They showed off exotic animals, while the surrounding fairground dazzled visitors. The golden age of circus lasted until the early 20th century.

Clowning around ▶
Clowns make fun of people and help us to see the silly side of things we all do. They developed from the 16th-century Italian *Commedia dell'arte* (artists' comedy), in which characters wore masks. English clown Joseph Grimaldi started the tradition of white-faced clowning in the early 1800s.

Amazing feats

Anyone with an unusual talent could make a living in the circus. The weirder the act, the more the public would pay. Phineas Barnum said of his customers, "There's a sucker born every minute."

• In 1860, Barnum showed the original **"Siamese twins"** Chang and Eng, who were joined at the chest. Both were married, and they had 22 children between them.

• The greatest high-wire artist of all time was Blondin. His most famous act was to cross Niagara Falls on a tightrope in 1859.

• The original Tom Thumb was 28 inches (71 cm) tall at the age of 22.

▲ **Ringling Brothers**
The Ringling family started a circus in 1884, but they were not successful until they bought an elephant four years later. By 1907, the Ringling Brothers had bought Barnum's famous circus and were the biggest show in the United States, with a tent seating 10,000 people.

In one traveling act, a man would swallow a lightbulb, which then glowed inside his body.

Falling Fast

A SLOW, NERVOUS CLIMB, a frightful pause at the top, then a wonderful, terrifying zoom downward. Nothing beats the thrill of a white-knuckle ride! A machine powers the cars up the first hill, but it is **gravity** that drives the rest of the swooping journey.

White-knuckle rides began as ice slides in 16th-century Russia. One of the first with wheeled cars was an existing railway for a mine, built in 1827 in Pennsylvania. Passengers soon took the place of coal in the cars on the Mauch Chunk Switchback Gravity Railroad, screaming in terror as they rode the 18-mile (29-km) track.

Roller coasters

In 1884, the first real roller coaster opened at Coney Island in New York. Cars traveled only at the speed of a running person. Soon higher, steeper wooden tracks were built to make rides faster— and scarier.

Would You Believe...?

Feel the force
The world's fastest roller coasters push riders down into their seats with a maximum force of 4 g (four times the force of gravity). This is a third greater than the g-force astronauts feel during the launch of a space shuttle. It is possible to build even faster rides, but the riders would pass out!

◀ **Ice slide**
Bored Russians amused themselves by plunging down wooden slides like this one from the 18th century. The "cars" were blocks of ice fitted with wooden seats. Even Russian empress Catherine the Great was a fan.

COOPER STREET, MANCHESTER.

▲ **A loopy ride**
Russian ice slides inspired small, wheeled
indoor rides like this "Centrifugal Railway,"
built in an old English theater in the 1850s.
Riders sitting in small carts whirled through
two loops on their way from the balcony
to the stage.

Steel rides ▶
The tight turns and
enormous speed of
rides today are possible
because they are made
from steel. Karl
Bacon designed
the first steel-tube
roller coaster,
Matterhorn Bobsleds,
which opened in
Disneyland in 1959.

Water Sports

OCEANS COVER TWO-THIRDS OF EARTH'S surface. Yet most of us have never spent more than a few moments under water at a time. Those who have, however, do not seem to want to come up out of the waves. They wriggle into rubber wet suits and strap on scuba gear—tanks of air that let them swim as free as fish for about 40 minutes at a time.

Scuba diving is one of the world's fastest growing sports, but this is just one way to have some wet fun. There are weirder and wackier water sports, too, such as free diving, extreme surfing, and waterfall plunges. In most of them, the thrill comes from the danger. The risk of drowning is never far away.

▼ Bog snorkeling
Imagine swimming through a wet, spongy bog. Amazingly, hundreds of people do. The world's bog-snorkeling championship takes place each summer at Llanwrtyd Wells in Great Britain.

The most daring free divers grip a heavy sledgehammer that drags them quickly into deep water.

Cave divers plunge into flooded caverns and tunnels. If anything goes wrong, they can't just swim to the surface. And free divers don't use scuba gear. They just hold their breath and plunge to depths of 390 feet (119 m).

▲ **Deep sea pioneer**
Macedonian king Alexander the Great was among the first to enjoy a visit under water. According to legend, he was lowered into the sea in a barrel in 332 B.C.

Would You Believe...? Would You Believe...? Would You Believe...?

Not a barrel of fun
In 1901, 63-year-old school teacher Annie Taylor climbed into a barrel and rolled over Niagara Falls. Climbing out at the bottom, she said "No one ought ever do that again." But she started an unofficial sport that has since killed a third of those who try it.

▲ **Extreme surfing**
For the ultimate big wave thrill, surfers get towed out to sea by a helicopter or Jet Ski. This allows them to ride waves bigger and faster than any they could paddle out to. Called tow-in surfing, this sport is not for the timid. Falling from these huge waves can crush surfers on rocks or hold them under water for up to a minute.

Taking to Air

First hang glider ▶
German Otto Lilienthal launched his bat-wing gliders from a home-made hill. After more than 200 safe flights, a gust of wind upset his craft in 1896, and he fell to his death.

SOARING HIGH ABOVE THE ground like a bird is a dream that has always enchanted people. In ancient Greek myths, Daedalus and his son Icarus made wings from wax and feathers. Icarus crashed when he flew too close to the sun and melted the wax. For centuries, most would-be birdmen were no more successful.

In the 11th century, a jump from a tower killed an English monk called Eilmer. Otto Lilienthal, inventor of the **hang glider,** died when one of his craft crashed. Wilbur and Orville Wright made flight safer when they perfected a flying machine in 1905.

The chance that a plane might crash during a daring stunt drew crowds to air shows.

Wing walking ▶
Early American flyers bought cheap surplus planes when World War I ended in 1918. Nicknamed **barnstormers,** they performed stunts like wing walking at small-town aviation shows.

Flying soon became a popular sport. Aircraft were little more than box kites with engines, and anyone with enough skill—and money—could build one. Rich and famous people bought planes and raced them or flew them for pleasure.

Thrill seekers

Today anyone can take to the sky after a few hang-gliding lessons, but simple flight is too tame for some. Serious thrill seekers **parachute** from towers or bridges, or they plunge from aircraft on surfboards.

Hang gliding ▲
Like Lilienthal, today's hang-glider pilots control their fragile, kite-like crafts by shifting their weight around in the harness that hangs from the wing.

BASE jumping ▶
You do not necessarily need an aircraft to use a parachute. BASE jumpers leap from places nearer the ground. BASE stands for the high spots the jumpers use: Buildings, Antennae, Spans (such as bridges), and Earth (cliffs). Because these launch points are relatively low, there is not very much time for the parachute to open, and the sport is very dangerous.

33

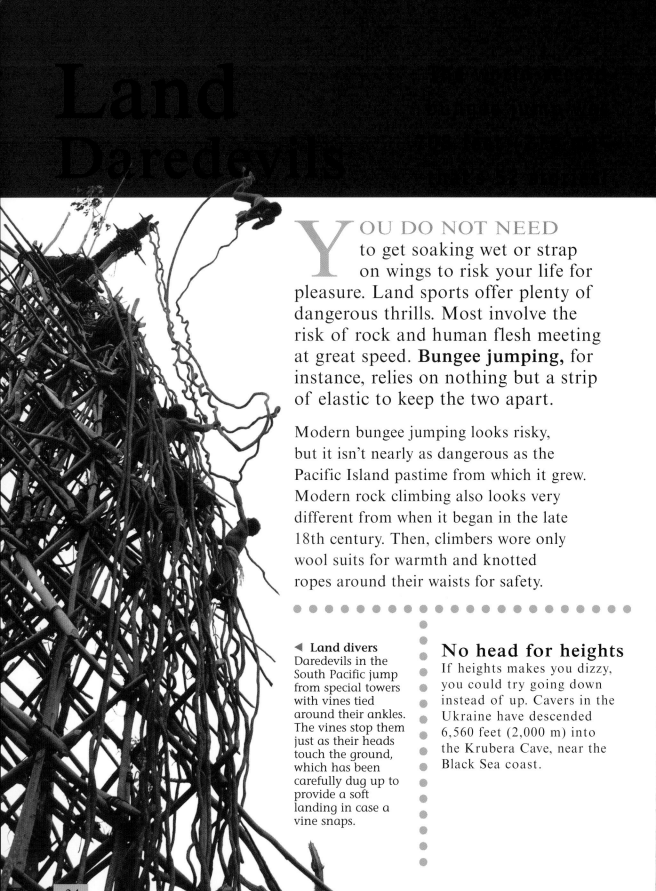

Land
Daredevils

YOU DO NOT NEED to get soaking wet or strap on wings to risk your life for pleasure. Land sports offer plenty of dangerous thrills. Most involve the risk of rock and human flesh meeting at great speed. **Bungee jumping,** for instance, relies on nothing but a strip of elastic to keep the two apart.

Modern bungee jumping looks risky, but it isn't nearly as dangerous as the Pacific Island pastime from which it grew. Modern rock climbing also looks very different from when it began in the late 18th century. Then, climbers wore only wool suits for warmth and knotted ropes around their waists for safety.

◀ **Land divers**
Daredevils in the South Pacific jump from special towers with vines tied around their ankles. The vines stop them just as their heads touch the ground, which has been carefully dug up to provide a soft landing in case a vine snaps.

No head for heights
If heights makes you dizzy, you could try going down instead of up. Cavers in the Ukraine have descended 6,560 feet (2,000 m) into the Krubera Cave, near the Black Sea coast.

34

Would You Believe...? Would You Believe...? Would You Believe...?

Party at the top?
Early in the history of rock climbing, local guides led wealthy climbers to mountain peaks. When English writer Albert Smith was led up Mont Blanc in France in 1851, his expedition took with them 96 bottles of wine. They celebrated with a picnic at the top—where Smith fell asleep.

Today, specialized equipment and high-performance clothing protect climbers. They still find ways to risk their lives in search of thrills, however, tackling crags and cliffs that early climbers would have thought impossible.

▶ **Vertical dancing**
Free climbing uses ropes only for protection against falls, not to help climbers get up the rock. The most daring and skilled form of free climbing is free soloing, in which climbers go up alone and without ropes to catch them.

Nice Ice

◀ **Speed skating**
Wearing clingy outfits and streamlined helmets that reduce air resistance, the best speed skaters circle an icy track at a frightening 28 miles per hour (45 kmph).

FROZEN WATER WILL turn any surface into a slide and make difficult sports, like rock climbing, even more of a challenge. Many of today's winter sports began for sensible reasons. Skating, for example, has allowed people to cross frozen rivers since 1000 B.C. Now these pastimes offer excitement that is hard to match in any other sport.

Ice hockey players use the slipperiness of the frozen rink to make their game the fastest team sport. Walloped by a speeding stick, the puck can fly across the ice at up to 120 miles per hour (193 kmph).

◀ **Ice climbing**
A frosty coating makes rock slippery, but it can also make impossible surfaces like waterfalls climbable. Climbers use boot spikes called crampons and specially shaped axes to grip the ice.

▲ **Origins of ice skating**
The people of Scandinavia were probably the first to go ice skating, using bone or antler skates to skid wildly across frozen rivers. These English bone skates are about 800 years old. Faster ice skates with metal blades were probably a Dutch invention from the 17th century.

The slopes that steep skiers use are so extreme that snow barely sticks to them.

Speed skiing is the fastest sport without a motor. Experts reach 150 miles per hour (241 kmph). They move so fast that their skis don't even touch the snow, and a fall causes burns as well as broken bones.

▼ **Bobsledding**
Bobsleds are a sleeker, faster, high-tech version of the sled. They hurtle down specially built ice tracks as fast as speeding cars. On the corners, the crews are pressed sideways at 5 g (five times the force of gravity).

Would You Believe...? Would You Believe...?

Exploration or sport?
When polar exploration began in about 1910, heroic adventurers risked their lives racing to these frozen frontiers. Today, anyone with $67,000 and 11 weeks to spare can ski across Antarctica to the South Pole. (The Arctic is more tricky, since some of the ice melts in summer.)

Flying and sliding
Ski fliers launch themselves from ramps in an extreme form of ski jumping. The best ski fliers travel nearly 800 feet (244 m), the length of 28 buses parked end to end. At least a bobsled offers some protection. Bobsled races began in 1884 in Switzerland and were first run on steep, narrow courses 20 years later.

Feats of Endurance

EATING INSECTS, running long distances, walking on fire: Challenges like these are grueling, painful, and downright dangerous. So why are they growing in popularity? Often people take part to prove that they can overcome fear and disgust or put up with pain and hardship.

In Europe, these feats of **endurance** probably began in the Middle Ages. Back then, people accused of crimes performed "ordeals" to prove that they were innocent. It was believed that these ordeals would not harm those who had done no wrong.

Locust

▲ **Eating bugs**
Food stunts on TV, such as eating dishes of caterpillars, are not all they seem. Many kinds of insects are edible, wholesome foods and contain as much protein as steak. In fact, insects make up an important part of the diet in some rural areas of Asia and Africa.

Games and shows
Today there's money and fame to be had in feats of endurance. Ordinary people can get on TV if they are willing to endure discomfort at best, and deadly danger at worst. And television audiences will tune in for a chance to watch celebrities do something that they find gross or humiliating.

▲ **Fire walking**
In many different societies around the world, people used to prove their religious faith or superhuman powers by walking on hot coals. Today, fire walking is a popular way to overcome fear. It is usually safe if feet and coals are correctly prepared. Some walkers still burn their feet, so never try this yourself!

▼ **Trial by ordeal**
Instead of a trial in court, some medieval defendants had to undergo the "trial by accursed morsel." The challenge was to eat a feather sandwich.

In the Middle Ages, a defendant could be forced to carry a hot metal bar to prove his innocence.

▲ **Endurance festival**
At Japanese universities, students have traditionally challenged each other to *Gaman Taikai* (tough-it-out) contests. A TV program in the 1980s called *Za Gaman* made the contests famous outside Japan. It also set the style for similar reality shows worldwide. The games are still popular in Japan. In the one shown here, people strip and splash ice-cold water on themselves.

Shall
We Dance?

A MUSICAL BEAT IS HARD TO resist. You just have to get on your feet and dance. Though today we do it mainly for pleasure, dancing has always been part of ancient rituals and religion. This is probably how dance began.

▲ **Ball-gown elegance**
This English couple from 1680 are dancing in the style that had recently become popular. The woman is hitching up her dress to show off her steps.

In Stone Age Europe, **shamans** (tribal sorcerers) may have been trying to bring hunters good luck when they dressed in animal skins. Their dancing steps imitated the beasts the hunters were seeking. Later dances were a form of worship.

The Italian dance *the tarantella* **began as a frantic** cure for **a spider bite.**

◄ **Whirling dervishes**
Spinning like a top is a form of worship for dervishes, members of a Turkish Muslim group called the Sufis. The dervishes believe their whirling around brings them closer to God.

◀ **Sri Lankan devil dance**
To help cure insanity, illness, or bad luck, Sri Lanka's devil dancers leap through the air and whirl flames. They aim to banish demons from their patients. Though the dancers are men, their costumes make them look half female.

In the 1930s, a dance marathon in Chicago went on for seven months.

Dirty dancing

Because it brings men and women close together, dancing has always had a bad reputation in some parts. In England, mixed dancing was labeled sinful in the 17th century. A century later, the **waltz** was thought distasteful in some places, though it is now completely respectable.

Elvis the Pelvis ▶

The hip-swinging dance movements of singer Elvis Presley earned him the nickname "the Pelvis." Presley's sexy shaking was too much for 1950s television audiences. When he appeared on a popular show, cameras filmed him only from the waist up.

● ● ● ● ● ● ● ● ● ● ● ● ● ● ● ● ● ●

In the 1920s and '30s in the United States, dance marathons kept out-of-work couples dancing day and night for weeks on end. The last couple to drop won a much-needed cash prize.

Celebrations
Around the Year

CHRISTMAS, NEW YEAR'S, Thanksgiving, and the Fourth of July—all add excitement to the calendar, but they are not the only events that help the year go round. Every day there's a festival going on somewhere. Tiny, weird, and wacky, some are hardly known outside the village that celebrates them. But others are major national holidays.

◀ **Shrove Tuesday**
Lent is a time when Christians traditionally give up certain foods. In the past, Christians who were not supposed to eat butter or eggs during Lent used them up in pancakes or pastries on Shrove Tuesday, the day before Lent begins.

Religion is the reason for many holidays. The more religions, the more festivals there are. India, which is home to Muslims, Hindus, Buddhists, Christians, Jains, and others, probably has more holidays than any other country.

The Burryman of Queensferry ▶
On a summer's day each year, a strange figure tours the Scottish town of Queensferry, collecting money in silence. He is covered in the seed pods of the burr thistle and has a rose crown. Townspeople believe that bad luck will follow if the Burryman stops making his annual tour.

Jack-o'-lanterns originally were meant to represent the souls of dead people. But who was Jack? According to Irish legend, Jack was a spirit banned from both heaven and hell. He was doomed to forever roam the earth with a dimly lit lantern.

Before Christianity became Europe's main religion, the passing of the seasons was a big reason to celebrate. To stop these pagan (non-Christian) festivities, Christians scheduled their holy days to fall on the same days. Many of today's Christian celebrations have pagan roots.

Halloween

The scariest day of the year came from a pagan holiday in Britain. November 1 was the Day of the Dead, when people left out food for their ancestors' ghosts. When Chritianity arrived, the church started All Saints' Day, or All Hallows', on this same date. The evening, or eve, before All Hallows' became All Hallows' Eve, known today as Halloween.

Scary masks remind us that Halloween was thought to be the day the dead came to life.

Day of the Dead ▶
Mexicans honor their ancestors with a joyful festival held around November 1st. Called *Día de los muertos* (Day of the Dead), it's a chance to visit graves, build small household **shrines**, and exchange grisly presents in the shape of skulls and skeletons. Many gifts are edible; bread and sugar treats are especially popular.

What's So Weird about That?

AS TIMES HAVE CHANGED, pastimes have changed—though sometimes less than you might expect. Gladiators no longer fight to the death, but you can still watch boxers beat each other senseless. The cruelest animal sports, such as bear baiting, are banned, but hunting and fishing are still popular.

So what's weird, and what's not? Things that seem normal now, such as music and dancing, were once outlawed. And to people from the past, today's extreme sports might seem pointlessly risky.

Would You Believe...? Would You Believe...?

A harmless game of golf?
Games and sports are not always as harmless as they seem. Golf doesn't have the bloody reputation of gladiator combat, but courses can ruin the environment. An 18-hole course uses as much water as a town of 10,000 people and can turn the surrounding land to desert.

◄ **Nothing new**
Spinning in a circular cage is one of the latest amusement park thrills—though the roller wheel in this picture is from 1927. Is anything really new in sports and recreation?

How weird is your favorite pastime?
Compared to the way you spend your free time, some of the pastimes in this book may seem very strange. But as long as what we do for sports and recreation doesn't harm others, does it really matter if it's weird and wacky—or just plain dumb?

"Old-fashioned" pastimes have a habit of reappearing with new names.

Find Out More

You can find out lots more about the strange and surprising history of sports and recreation from these books and websites.

Books

Horton, Ron. *Extreme Athletes*. Detroit: Lucent Books, 2005.

Leavitt, Caroline. *Samurai*. Mankato, Minn.: Capstone Press, 2006.

Malam, John. *Gladiator: Life and Death in Ancient Rome*. New York: DK, 2002.

Morley, Jacqueline. *How to Be an Ancient Greek Athlete*. Washington, D.C.: National Geographic, 2005.

Pellowski, Michael. *The Little Giant Book of Football Facts*. New York: Sterling, 2005.

Rappoport, Ken. *Ladies First: Women Athletes Who Made a Difference*. Atlanta: Peachtree, 2005.

Rosenthal, Paul. *America at Bat: Baseball Stuff & Stories*. Washington, D.C.: National Geographic, 2002.

Salkeld, Audrey. *Climbing Everest: Tales of Triumph and Tragedy on the World's Highest Mountain*. Washington, D.C.: National Geographic, 2003.

Van Steenwyk, Elizabeth. *Let's Go to the Beach: A History of Sun and Fun by the Sea*. New York: Henry Holt, 2001.

Websites

Toys and games
http://www.historychannel.com/exhibits/toys/index.html
Find out how some of your favorite toys and games started on this interactive site.

Gladiators
http://www.bbc.co.uk/history/ancient/romans/launch_gms_gladiator.shtml#
This site challenges you to equip a virtual gladiator with the correct weapons and armor, then send him into a virtual arena to meet his fate.

Jousting
http://www.tudorbritain.org/joust
A medieval battle game that lets you relive the thrills and spills of the tournament.

Roller coasters
http://virtual.questacon.edu.au/rollercoaster
Build a virtual roller coaster, then race around it in a dizzying ride!

Ball games
http://www.ballgame.org
A spectacular interactive Web site about the famous ball game of Central America. Find out what the players wore, learn the rules, then play the game.

Sports and Games Museum
http://americanhistory.si.edu/collections/subject_detail.cfm?key=32&colkey=29
Browse an online exhibit that includes Muhammad Ali's boxing gloves and the first Nintendo Game Boy.

Circus Legends
http://www.ringling.com/explore/history/legend/legend.aspx
Read about the most memorable performers and the most amazing acts in the history of the Ringling Brothers and Barnum & Bailey Circus.

Glossary

armor protective clothing, often made of metal, worn in battle to prevent injuries

Aztecs people who ruled Mexico before it was conquered by Spanish explorers in the 16th century

barnstormer a skilled aircraft pilot who performs flying tricks for a living

BASE jumping the sport of jumping off high places, such as bridges, with a parachute

blood sport any sport that involves killing animals

bungee jumping the sport of jumping from high points with an elastic rope tied to the legs to break the fall

crest a decorative design on a knight's helmet

endurance the ability to put up with pain, hardship, or digust for a long period of time

gambler a person who makes a deal (called a bet) with another person about an unpredictable event, in which the one who correctly guesses the result wins money from the other

game any wild animal that is traditionally hunted for food

gladiator a person who participated in death matches as a form of entertainment in ancient Rome

gravity a natural force that pulls together heavy objects. Gravity is the force that makes things fall downward on Earth.

hang glider a one-person aircraft without an engine that glides on moving air like a kite

joust to wage a fake battle on horseback using a long pole-like weapon called a lance to topple an opponent

lance a long, blunt pole used by jousting knights to knock each other from their horses

mantrap a trap used to catch a person who is trespassing, or illegally going, on private property

marathon a long running race inspired by an ancient Greek messenger. A marathon is 26 miles and 385 yards (42 km).

martial arts fighting methods that originated in Asia. Martial arts have often ancient roots and focus on fighting without weapons.

Mayans people who ruled Central America and part of Mexico until Spanish conquest in the 16th century

Olympic Games an international sports contest held every four years in summer and winter; a similar event held in ancient Greece

Pan-American Games an international sports contest, modeled after the Olympic Games, just for countries in North and South America

parachute a device used by people jumping from great heights to break their fall. A parachute opens into a large, umbrella-like object that fills with air.

philosophy the study of knowledge, thought, and the basic ideas of right and wrong

sacrifice the killing of a person or animal in a way that was meant to please a god

shaman a non-Christian priest believed to possess powers, such as the ability to foretell the future, cure illness, or control the weather

shrine a small place of worship, often found in a home

Siamese twins twins born joined together

snorkeling swimming underwater while breathing through a curved tube that extends into the air

Vikings Scandinavian people who sailed as pirates from 800 to 1050 A.D.

waltz a graceful dance in which men and women perform matching steps with their bodies held close together

Index

A

acrobatics, 26
airplanes, 32, 33
Africa, 23, 38
Alexander the Great, 31
All Hallows' Day, 43
American Indians, 9, 15
amusement park, 44
ancient Egypt, 4, 5, 16
ancient Greece, 5, 14, 32
ancient Rome, 5, 6–7, 10, 16, 21, 22, 23
animals, 4, 5, 6, 20–21, 22–23, 24–25, 26, 40, 44
Antarctica, 37
archaeologists, 4
Arctic, 37
armor, 6, 7, 8, 9, 12, 46
Asia, 12, 38
Astley, Philip, 26
astragals, 5
astronauts, 19, 28
Athens, 14
Aztecs, 4, 8, 17, 46

B

Bacon, Karl, 29
badgers, 24
balls, 3, 4, 5, 16–17, 18–19
barnstormers, 32, 46
Barnum, Phineas T., 26, 27
BASE jumping, 3, 33, 46
battles, 3, 6, 8, 9, 10, 22
bear baiting, 22, 44
betting, 20, 21
Bibby, Jackie, 38
billiards, 10
birdmen, 32
Black Death, 41

Blondin, 27
blood sports, 25, 46
bobsledding, 37
bog snorkeling, 3, 30
bowling, 19
boxing, 10, 44
Buddhism, 42
bull vaulting, 22
bungee jumping, 34, 46
Burryman, 42

C

Calcio Storico, 18
camels, 20, 21
caterpillars, 38
Catherine the Great, 28
Catholics, 42
cattle, 5
cave diving, 31
caving, 34
celebrations, 42–43
Central America, 16, 17
Centrifugal Railway, 29
chariot racing, 6, 21
Christians, 42, 43
circuses, 26–27
clowns, 26
cock fighting, 23
cockroaches, 21
Commedia dell'arte, 26
computer games, 3, 6, 8
Coney Island, 28
coup, 9
Cousteau, Jacques, 30
crests, 9, 46

DE

Daedalus, 32
dance marathon, 41
dancing, 40–41, 44
danger, 3, 28, 30, 33, 38
Day of the Dead, 43
deer, 24
demons, 41
dervishes, 40
devils, 41

dice, 5
Disneyland, 29
diving, 30–31
dog fighting, 23
dogs, 23, 24, 25
dolls, 4
dueling, 10–11, 12
Eilmer, 32
elephants, 27
endurance, 38–39, 46
expulsim ludere, 16
extinction, 23

FG

fairground, 26
fans, 16
fencing, 11
festivals, 5, 42–43
fighting, 3, 6, 7, 8–9, 10–11, 12–13, 18, 19, 22–23
fire walking, 38
fishing, 44
fitness, 12
flowery wars, 8
flying, 3, 32–33
follis, 16
football, 6, 18–19
fox hunting, 24
foxes, 24
free climbing, 35
free diving, 30, 31
free soloing, 35
frogs, 21
g-force, 28
Gagnan, Émile, 30
Gaman Taikai, 39
gamblers, 20, 21, 23, 46
Germany, 14
gladiators, 6, 7, 22, 46 23, 44
gliders, 32, 33, 46
God 10
golf, 19, 44
graffiti, 6
gravity, 28, 37, 46
Grimaldi, Joseph, 26
guns, 12

HIJK

Halloween, 43
handball, 16
hang gliders, 3, 32, 33
harpastum, 16
hawks, 24, 25
helicopters, 31
Hinduism, 42
hockey, 36
holidays, 42–43
Hopi Indians, 4
hoplomachus, 7
horses, 3, 9, 20, 21, 24, 25, 26
hounds, 25
hunting, 3, 24–25, 40, 44
Icarus, 32
ice, 3, 36–37
ice climbing, 36
ice skating, 36
ice slides, 28
insects, 38
Internet, 20
Islam, 42
jack-o'-lanterns, 43
Jainism, 42
Japan, 12, 13, 39
jockeys, 21
jousting, 8, 9, 46
judo, 12
jujitsu, 12
kachina, 4
kangaroo, 26
karate, 12, 13
kata, 13
kings, 3, 24
kites, 33
knattleikr, 17
knights, 8, 9, 25
Korea, 12

LMN

lances, 8, 9, 46
land divers, 34
Lent, 42

Léotard, Jules, 26
Lilienthal, Otto, 32
lions, 22, 26
locusts, 38
losing, 7, 16
Macedonia, 31
mantrap, 24, 46
marathon, 14, 15, 46
marbles, 5
martial arts, 12–13, 46
Matterhorn Bobsleds, 29
Mauch Chunk Switchback Gravity Railroad, 28
Mayans, 16, 17, 19, 46
medieval, 24, 25, 39, 41
messengers, 14, 15
Middle Ages, 24, 38, 39
Minoans, 22
Mont Blanc, 35
moon, 19
movies, 12
munera, 6
murmillo, 7
music, 40, 44
Muslims, 40
NASA, 19
Nazis, 14
New Jersey, 18
New York, 15, 28
Niagara Falls, 27, 31
Nomlaki, 15

ostriches, 3, 21
Owens, Jesse, 14
pagans, 43
Pan-American Games, 8, 46
pancakes, 42
parachutes, 33, 46
Persians, 14
Pheidippides, 14
philosophy, 12, 46
pigs, 3, 5, 21, 24
pistols, 11–12
Plains Indians, 9
poaching, 24, 46
*pok-a-tok ,*16, 17, 19
polar exploration, 37
Presley, Elvis, 41
Pujol, Joseph, 26
rabbits, 25
racing, 3, 5, 14–15, 20–21, 37
racism, 14
rats, 23
religion, 4, 5, 38, 42, 43
retiarius, 6, 7
Ringling Brothers, 27
robots, 21
rock climbing, 34–35
roller coasters, 28–29
Roosevelt, Theodore, 19
rubber, 16, 17, 19
rules, 10, 16
running, 14–15, 38
Russia, 21, 28, 29

Scandinavia, 36
scuba, 30, 31
secutor, 6
self-defense, 12
shamans, 40, 46
Shepard, Allan, 19
shrines, 43, 46
Shrove Tuesday, 42
Siamese twins, 27, 46
Sicily, 16
ski flying, 37
ski jumping, 37
skiing, 3, 36, 37
slaves, 3, 6, 21
Smith, Albert, 35
snails, 20, 21
snakes, 38
soccer, 18, 21
soldiers, 9
South Pacific, 34
South Pole, 37
speed skating, 36
spiders, 40
sprinting, 14, 15
stadiums, 14
Stone Age, 40
stunts, 32
Sufis, 40
sumai, 12, 13
sumo wrestling, 12, 13
Super Bowl, 19
surfing, 30, 31
swimming, 21, 30
swords, 11, 12, 24

television, 3, 38, 39, 41
thrills, 21, 28, 30, 31, 33, 34, 35, 44
tigers, 22
tightropes, 26, 27
Tom Thumb, 27
tombs, 4
tournaments, 9
tow-in surfing, 31
toys, 4, 16
trapeze, 26
Ukraine, 34
Vikings, 17, 46
volleyball, 16

WXYZ

waltz, 41, 46
warfare, 8, 12
warriors, 6, 8, 12
water sports, 30–31
waterfalls, 30, 36
weapons, 6, 8, 9, 10
wheels, 4, 28, 29
wing walking, 32
wings, 32, 33, 34
winning, 5, 16, 21, 41
wolves, 24
World War I, 32
worship, 22, 25, 40
wrestling, 10, 13
Wright, Orville, 32
Wright, Wilbur, 32
Za Gaman 39

OPQR

Olympic Games 5, 10, 14, 15, 21, 46
ordeals, 38, 39

S

sacrifices, 5, 8, 16, 46
saints, 42
Samurai, 12

TUV

tae kwon do, 12
tarantella, 40
Taylor, Annie, 31

Picture credits

The publisher would like to thank the following for their kind permission to reproduce their photographs:

Position key: c=center; b=bottom; l=left; r=right; t=top

Front cover: Getty Images/Photodisc.

1: The Art Archive/Archaeological Museum Copan Honduras/ Dagli Orti; 4c: George H H Huey/Corbis; 4cr: Sawyers Photographic; 5cr: Sawyers Photographic; 5t The British Museum/Heritage Images; 6b: Ann Ronan Picture Library/Heritage; 7c: The British Museum/Heritage Images; 8br: Reuters/Corbis; 9b: David Cheskins/Pa/Empics; 10br: The British Museum/Heritage Images; 11c: The Board of Trustess of the Armouries/Heritage Images; 12r: Asaian Art 7 Archaeology, inc/Corbis; 13tr: Reuters/Corbis; 13c: Franco Vogt/Corbis; 14cl: Hulton-Deutsch/Corbis; 15b: Mary Altaffer/Ap/Empics; 16bl: The Art Archive/Dagli Orti; 16cr: The Art Archive/Dagli Orti; 17c: Akg-Images/Francois Guenet; 18tl: The Art Archive/Domencia Del Corriere/Dagli Orti; 18br: The Bridgeman Art Library; 19br: Bettmann/Corbis; 20b: Craig Lovell/Corbis; 20tr: Sawyers Photographic; 21cl: Reuters/Corbis; 22tr: The British Library/Heritage Images; 22b: The British Museum/Heritage Images; 23c: Swim Ink 2, llc/Corbis; 23tl: Sawyers Photographic; 23tc: Sawyers Photographic; 24bl: Ann Ronan Picture Library/Heritage; 24bc: The Board of Trustess of the Armouries/Heritage Images; 25r: Staffan Widstrand/Corbis; 27tl: Corbis; 27cr: The National Archives/Heritage Images; 28bl: Historical Picture Archives/Corbis; 29c: Rui Vieira/Pa/Empics; 29tr: Science Museum Pictorial; 30b: Benjamin Stansall/Epa/Corbis; 31cr: Rick Doyle/Corbis; 31tl: The British Library/Heritage Images; 32b: Bettmann/Corbis; 32tr: Oxford Science Archive/Heritage Images; 33r: Shamshahrin Shamsudin/Epa/Corbis; 34l: Anders Ryman/Corbis; 35c: Stefan Schuetz/Zefa/Corbis; 36l: Sportschrome/Empics; 36cr: Museum of London/Heritage Images; 37c: Matthias Rietschel/Ap/Empics; 38bl: Stapleton Collection/Corbis; 39c: Issei Kato/Reuters/Corbis; 39tl: Sawyers Photographic; 40bl: Archivo Iconographico, S.A./Corbis; 41r: Bettmann/Corbis; 42br: Homer Sykes/Alamy; 42cl: Sawyers Photographic; 43r: J Marshall-Tribaleye Images/Alamy: 43 c: Sawyers Photographic; 44bl: Mary Evans Picture Library